HIC! OR THE ENTIRE HISTORY OF WINE (ABRIDGED)

JULIAN CURRY

ILLUSTRATED BY CHRIS DUGGAN

VINUM BONUM

We couldn't have done it without help from

Michele Costa-Lukis who directed the live show and

Hugh Johnson who drank the Steinwein.

Special thanks also to copy editor Rosemary Furber,
to Elizabeth Ray and Baroness Wolfenden for kind permission
to publish their own and their late husbands' work,
to The Random House Group, and A.P. Watt Ltd. on behalf of the
Trustees of the Wodehouse Estate, for permission to publish
extracts from My Man Jeeves and The Code of the Woosters, and to
Lilliput Press for permission to publish an extract from John Ryan's
Remembering How We Stood. And to John Mortimer, John Stimpfig,
Hamish MacGibbon, Trevor Bowen, Gawn Grainger, Henry Simon,
Peter Langridge and many others who have been brilliantly
supportive, and/or whose work has been subtly plundered.

Design by Janet Folland.

First published in 2001 by Vinum Bonum
11 Hilly Fields Crescent, London SE4 1QA
hic@onetel.net.uk.
Printed by E H V Printers Ltd, London.

Text and illustrations copyright © 2001
Julian Curry and Chris Duggan.

The right of Julian Curry and Chris Duggan to be identified as the authors of this work
has been asserted in accordance with the Copyright, Designs and Patents Act 1988.
A catalogue record of this book is available from the British Library.

ISBN 0-9541050-0-1

FOREWORD

Julian Curry is a highly accomplished actor who played the opera-loving barrister and wine buff Claude Erskine-Brown in the Rumpole stories. Rumpole's consumption of wine is confined to the somewhat rough claret on sale in Pommeroy's Wine Bar, which he refers to as either 'Château Fleet Street' or, when in more censorious mood, 'Château Thames Embankment'. When Claude chatters on about tasting 'sunlight trapped in a bottle' and recognizing the vineyard on the correct side of the Gironde, Rumpole thinks, with momentary distaste, of 'the bit of barren soil between the cowshed and the pissoir, where the Château Pommeroy grape struggles for existence'.

So here is a scene about different approaches to wine. Rumpole, impatient with high-flown prose about aftertastes and the wine's nose, traces of raspberries and pepper and, horror of horrors, the spitting out of mouthfuls of good wine, sees his glass of Château Fleet Street as an anaesthetic against attacks by hostile judges and a path to mild oblivion. The point of wine, he tells Erskine-Brown, is surely to make yourself drunk.

Between snobbery and intoxication the great pleasures of drinking can be found. Wine is a healthy drink produced by the fruits of the earth, with a fascinating history, an important place in literature and is at the heart of the celebration of the Christian religion. Julian Curry has devised an entertaining one-man show, with scholarship lightly worn and some of the best jokes and literary celebrations included. By popular demand the text has been extended, printed and beautifully and comically illustrated by Chris Duggan.

You can read here about a 421 year old bottle of Steinwein from Germany, Churchill's champagne at breakfast, the blind monk Dom Pérignon and the wife divorced because her illicit love-making in the cellar shook the Château d'Yquem and disturbed the wine. You can hear from Jeeves on hangovers and Keats on the draught of vintage which can make you leave the mundane world and fade into the 'forest dim'. You can hear from Falstaff on sherry sack and Ovid, who said wine makes us fit for passion. The whole subject, and this book, are clearly presided over by the Great God of Wine, who was also known as the 'Betesticled' and 'The Great Remover of Inhibitions'.

To Julian Curry's fine anthology I would add this stanza from Byron's *Don Juan*, written after a heavy night:

> *'I would to heaven that I were so much to clay,*
> *As I am blood, bone, marrow, passion, feeling -*
> *Because at least the past were pass'd away -*
> *And for the future - (but I write this reeling*
> *Having got drunk exceedingly today*
> *So that I seem to stand upon the ceiling)*
> *I say - the future is a serious matter -*
> *And so for God's sake - hock and soda water!'*

But there is more in this book than hock and soda water. There is Latour, Lafite and Château Mouton, and much else to make up a fine, vintage entertainment.

John Mortimer.

PREFACE

As an actor and a wine nut, I've always relished opportunities to combine the two. In the TV series *Rumpole of the Bailey* for example, my character Claude Erskine-Brown finds himself in a blissfully silly scene, criticising a wine's 'nose' to Horace Rumpole, who misunderstands and indignantly defends his own nose. Heaven.

So when a friend suggested I should write myself a wine entertainment, he opened the door to a true labour of love. I became a bookworm, poring over vinous volumes, chuckling at liquorish limericks and wiping away a furtive tear at the romance and legend of wine. The result was *Hic!* or *The Entire History of Wine* (*abridged*). It is a cocktail: a light-hearted, live, one-man show, blending wine fact, fantasy, legend and humour, laced with generous tasting samples from famous authors.

What follows here is the performance script, more or less, of *Hic!* As for turning it into a book (an eminence to which it never aspired) the blame lies entirely with Chris Duggan. He produced one brilliant cartoon after another to accompany the text, until we had no choice but to go out looking for a printer.

Why more or less? Because this text is longer. For live performance I trimmed many of the quotes, to keep the show moving along at a good lick. Some cuts are now restored. As is Lord Cockburn's colourful account of the 'cravat lous'ner'.

Cheers!

JC

IN THE BEGINNING

A barrel of wine can work more miracles than a church full of saints.
Italian proverb.

I hadn't the heart to touch my breakfast. I told Jeeves to drink it himself.
P.G.Wodehouse.

The juice of the grape is the liquid quintessence of concentrated sunbeams.
Thomas Love Peacock.

Dionysus the Greek Wine God was always a popular deity. He was 'The Bull-horned God', 'The Betesticled', 'The Great Remover of Inhibition'. His worshippers were mainly women, known as Maenads. He led them in drunken frenzies, in riotous ecstatic dancing in the mountains. When Pentheus King of Thebes tried to stop the worship of Dionysus, legend says he was torn to pieces by the Maenads in their orgiastic fury. The power of wine!

Euripides wrote a play about these events, *The Bacchae*, in which I played the blind prophet Tiresias at the National Theatre in London. I wore a loin cloth, white contact lenses to suggest blindness, and false breasts. According to legend Tiresias had been a woman in an earlier part of his life. Unfortunately the contact lenses blurred my view of the naked Maenads as they danced around on stage. Otherwise I was happy in my work. Here's a taste of it:

> *We wash our souls, our parched,*
> *Aching souls in streams of wine and enter*
> *Sleep and oblivion. Filled with this good gift*
> *Mankind forgets its grief. But wine is more!*
> *It is the sun that comes after winter, the power*
> *That nudges earth awake. Dionysus comes alive in us.*
> *We soar, we fly, we shed the heavy clods of earth*
> *That weigh down the ethereal man.*

To the ancient Greeks, wine was an inspiration, a food, an indispensible medicine ... and a recreation. *Kottabos* was a popular after-dinner game. A small bronze disc called the 'plastinx' is delicately perched on a spindle, about the height of a standard lamp. Another much larger disc (the 'manes') is fixed half way down the stand. The aim of the game is to throw your wine dregs and hit the plastinx, making it fall with a clang onto the manes. *Kottabos*! You can imagine the Bertie Woosters and Gussie Fink-Nottles of ancient Greece relaxing after a banquet on a pile of cushions, farting and hiccupping contentedly, and hurling their dregs at the plastinx.

But wait a minute. Where and when did wine begin? Who invented it? Scientists believe that the earliest vines were grown about 5000 years before Christ in lush foothills south of Georgia, in the middle-eastern region of Caucasia. This just happens to agree with the Book of Genesis, since Noah's ark came to rest on Mount Ararat, itself in the Caucasus. There, as soon as he'd unloaded his animals, the Bible tells us, he *'began to be an husbandman, and he planted a vineyard: and he drank of the wine, and was drunken'*.

Two by Two

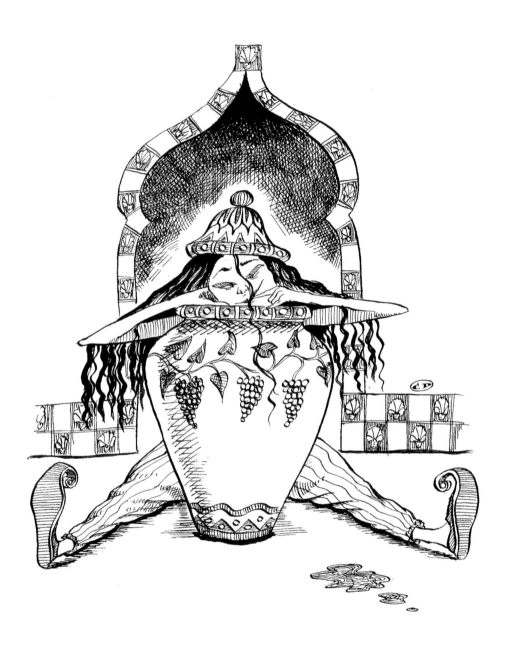

But wine no doubt invented itself. A ripe grape is a very sweet fruit. It contains up to one third sugar balanced by fresh-tasting acid, and it carries yeast on its skin. If left to its own devices, it may well ferment spontaneously, and become wine. And what is fermentation? Put simply, it's the conversion of sugar into alcohol and carbon dioxide, by the action of yeast.

The chemical formula for this ... By the way, in the court of the Persian King Jamsheed, grapes were stored in huge jars. Legend has it that one of the jars developed a peculiar smell, and the contents started foaming. It was put aside as unfit to eat, very likely poisonous. A lady of the harem was in a fit of black depression. Everybody was on top of her. I'm so sorry: every*thing* was on top of her. She decided to end her life by drinking from the jar. But yes ... you got there first! Instead of dying, she became miraculously exhilarated, and then enjoyed a restful sleep. Dutifully she told the king, and a quantity of wine was made, and Jamsheed and his court drank of the new beverage.

From Caucasia, barrels of wine were taken in coracles down the rivers Tigris and Euphrates to Babylon and Ur. Taste for wine and the knowledge of how to make it spread from the east, along with our civilisation. *'The peoples of the Mediterranean'* (this is the historian Thucydides) *'the peoples of the Mediterranean began to emerge from barbarism when they learnt to cultivate the olive and the vine.'* The Romans proceeded to spread the vine throughout their vast empire.

Wine is the flower in the buttonhole of civilisation!
Werumens Benning.

Some weasel took the cork out of my lunch!
W.C.Fields.

Wine gives courage, and makes men apt for passion!
Ovid.

In preparing this volume, I came across acres of good stuff. Some of it had me falling about.

My wife ... take my wife ... when in France my wife likes to be Chablis treated!

I say I say I say! I thought the bag-in-a-box was my deceased mother-in-law ... until I discovered the Australian Bladder Pack!

What do you get if you drink a German wine too fast? ... Hockups!

THE INCREDIBLY ANCIENT BOTTLE

I soon realised that there is enough material for a hundred such diversions. I'd have to narrow the field. Instead of The Entire History of Wine, I'm going to tell you a story. The very remarkable, true story of a single bottle. The oldest bottle of wine ever drunk. I first encountered it in Hugh Johnson's brilliant book, *The Story of Wine*.

London. July 7th, 1961. The offices of Ehrmann's the wine merchants. A small group of expert tasters gathers. They are about to sample a truly extraordinary bottle: a bottle of Steinwein, vintage 1540. A white wine from Germany, made 421 years earlier. What on earth will it be like? Its grapes were picked, pressed and fermented in the year King Henry VIII married the fifth of his wives, the delectable Catherine Howard. Is there the remotest possibility that it will still be drinkable?

It was unique. There is no record of any wine of comparable age being drunk. But what of other ancient bottles, probably long since dead, possibly still containing frail but exquisite taste sensations ... vinous shrouds of Turin?

The doyen of English wine-tasters is Michael Broadbent, a man whose nose has the sensitivity of a Stradivarius. He has written about 200 year old bottles from 1784, said to be the greatest vintage of the period. Of the Château d'Yquem he writes: *'Amber coloured, bright and lively. Scented vanilla, blancmange. Still sweet, perfect weight, balance and acidity. Flavour of peaches and cream, dry finish.'* Of the Château Lafite, on the other hand: *'Astounding smell, pure balsamic vinegar. Still sweet, intense, but alas, not drinkable.'*

Expensive Vinegar

Jancis Robinson tells of a bottle embossed 'Th. J.' found lying behind a wall in Paris. Thomas Jefferson, when he was American ambassador to France, became a connoisseur and collector of fine French wines. *If you have tears, prepare to shed them now!* She describes how Christies sold a single bottle of 1787 Château Lafite to the late Malcolm Forbes for a world record price of ... wait for it ... £105,000. This would have worked out at about £15,000 a glass had anyone actually drunk the wine, but Forbes chose to put the famous bottle on a suitably antique table in his Jefferson Museum, beside a model of the great man. There it stood for many months, duly revered, until someone noticed that the heat from a nearby spotlight must have shrivelled the cork, which had dropped into the wine, allowing it to spoil under the full force of oxygen. Thus did the world's most expensive bottle of wine become the world's most expensive bottle of vinegar.

HAVE SOME MADEIRA, M'DEAR!

The longest-lived and most resilient of wines is madeira. They recently dug up a 317 year old bottle in Spitalfields. It was said to be *'fresh, lively and palatable'*. It is not so trendy nowadays, but it was very fashionable in the 18th and 19th centuries. In America it was chosen to be served on the occasion of the Declaration of Independence.

So, what's the big deal? It's fortified with brandy, as are port and sherry. What makes it unique is, it's also baked. The island of Madeira ... By the way, did you know it was discovered in 1418 by a Portuguese sea captain called Zarco the Cross-eyed? Was he cross-eyed before or after he'd been at the grog? Who can tell ... But it's way out in the Atlantic, Madeira, 500 miles off the coast of Morocco. It soon became a natural port of call on sea trade routes. Before long its wine was a standard part of ships' cargoes, travelling round the world, crossing the equator, being subjected to treatment that would turn any other wine to vinegar. Miraculously madeira turned out a great deal better after the effects of baking tropical heat. Isn't that romantic?

The process is evoked by Charles Dickens in *Dombey and Son*:

Solomon Gills looked a little graver as he finished his dinner, and glanced from time to time at the boy's bright face. When dinner was done, and the cloth was cleared away (the entertainment had been brought from a neighbouring eating-house), he lighted a candle, and went down below into a little cellar, while his nephew, standing on the mouldy staircase, dutifully held the light. After a moment's groping here and there, he presently returned with a very ancient-looking bottle, covered with dust and dirt.

'Why uncle Sol!' said the boy, 'what are you about! That's the wonderful madeira - there's only one more bottle!'

Uncle Sol nodded his head, implying that he knew very well what he was about; and having drawn the cork in solemn silence, filled two glasses and set the bottle and a third clean glass on the table.

'You shall drink the other bottle, Wally,' he said to his nephew, 'when you have come to good fortune; when you are a thriving, respected, happy man; when the start in life you have made today shall have brought you, as I pray heaven it may! - to a smooth part of the course you have to run, my child. My love to you!'

Some of the fog that hung about old Sol seemed to have got into his throat; for he spoke huskily. His hand shook too, as he clinked his glass against his nephew's. But having once got the wine to his lips, he tossed it off like a man, and smacked them afterwards.

'Dear uncle,' said the boy, affecting to make light of it, while the tears stood in his eyes, 'for the honour you have done me, et cetera et cetera. I shall now beg to propose Mr Solomon Gills with three times three and one cheer more. Hurrah! and you'll return thanks Uncle, when we drink the last bottle together; won't you?'

They clinked their glasses again; and Walter, who was hoarding his wine, took a sip of it, and held the glass up to his eye with as critical an air as he could possibly assume ...

Solomon Gills rubbed his hands with an air of stealthy enjoyment, as he talked of the sea, and looked on the seafaring objects about him with an air of inexpressible complacency.

'Think of this wine for instance,' said old Sol, 'which has been to the East Indies and back, I'm not able to say how often, and has been once round the world. Think of the pitch-dark nights, the roaring winds, and rolling seas ...'

'The thunder, lightning, rain, hail, storm of all kinds,' said the boy.

'To be sure,' said Solomon, 'that this wine has passed through. Think what a straining and creaking of timbers and masts ... what a whistling and howling of the gale through ropes and rigging.'

'What a clambering aloft of men, vying with each other who shall lie out first upon the yards ... to furl the icy sails, while the ship rolls and pitches like mad!' cried his nephew.

'Exactly so,' said Solomon, 'has gone on over the old cask that held this wine. Why, when the Charming Sally went down in the ... '

'In the Baltic Sea, in the dead of night ... five and twenty minutes past twelve when the captain's watch stopped in his pocket ... he lying dead against the mainmast ... on the fourteenth of February, 1749!' cried Walter, with great animation.

'Aye, to be sure!' cried old Sol, 'quite right! Then, there were 500 casks of such wine aboard; and all hands (except the first mate, first lieutenant, two seamen and a lady, in a leaky boat) going to work to stave the casks, got drunk and died drunk, singing "Rule Britannia", when she settled and went down, ending with one awful scream in chorus.'

BOCKSBEUTELS AND BON VIVEURS

Where was I? Ah yes. The Steinwein. Der Steinwein! Stein is the best vineyard in Würzburg, in Franconia. *'Send me a few bottles of wine from Würzburg,'* wrote Goethe to his wife, *'as no other wine tastes good in comparison.'* It is said that Franconia wines hammer into the mouth, grab the drinker's tongue and pummel it. Instead of the familiar tall, thin flutes, their bottles are flagons called 'Bocksbeutels', which is German for a billy goat's scrotum. Not a lot of people know that. One swig from a Bocksbeutel can bring tears to your eyes.

The local weather is notorious for extremes. Forty in the shade is not uncommon. 1540 was an *annus mirabilis*. It was a meteorological prodigy, a freak. The summer was so hot and dry that the Rhine dried up, and people rode across the river bed on horseback. They say it was the greatest vintage for 1000 years. In the Burgerspital in Würzburg, a phenomenal and stunning wine was made. It must have combined great sweetness with exceptional alcoholic strength. It was a legend.

A magnificently carved cask was specially built to contain it, in which our wine enjoys a long sleep, while waiting to be bottled. This will not be possible for some 200 years.

15
40

Do
Not
Disturb

The Sleeping Beauty

During which time Shakespeare is born and creates the spectacular bon viveur, Sir John Falstaff:

A good sherris sack hath a two-fold operation in it. It ascends me into the brain, dries me there all the foolish and dull and crudy vapours which environ it; makes it apprehensive, quick, forgetive, full of nimble, fiery and delectable shapes, which, deliver'd o'er to the voice, the tongue, which is the birth, becomes excellent wit. The second property of your excellent sherris is, the warming of the blood; which before cold and settled, left the liver white and pale, which is the badge of pusillanimity and cowardice, but the sherris warms it and makes it course from the inwards to the parts extreme. It illumineth the face, which as a beacon gives warning to all the rest of this little kingdom, man, to arm; and then the vital commoners and inland petty spirits muster me all to their captain, the heart, who, great and puffed up with this retinue, doth any deed of courage; and this valour comes of sherris. Skill in the weapon is nothing without sack for that sets it a-work; and learning, a mere hoard of gold kept by a devil till sack commences it and sets it in act and use. Hereof comes it that Prince Harry is valiant; for the cold blood he did naturally inherit of his father, he hath, like lean, sterile and bare land, manured, husbanded, and tilled, with excellent endeavour of drinking good and good store of fertile sherris, that he is become very hot and valiant. If I had a thousand sons, the first human principle I should teach them should be, to forswear thin potations and addict themselves to sack.

The long reign of Queen Elizabeth I comes to an end.

Shakespeare dies.

It is 1640, and the Steinwein has been slumbering peacefully in its barrel for 100 years, waiting for the evolution of corks and bottles.

A lovely, romantic scenario, but impossible! Even on the most unlikely hypothesis that nobody drank any of it during those 100 years, the wine would have evaporated and spoiled. Because a barrel is not completely airtight in the way a bottle is. There is a very gradual, very slight ullage, meaning loss of its contents by seepage into the wood and away into the atmosphere. In Cognac they call this lost liquor 'La part des anges'. The angels' share. So what happened?

The custom was to keep such special casks topped up with a newer vintage of similar wine. Another possibility is that stones were dropped in through the bung hole to fill the gap. Or maybe the wine was transferred to a smaller cask, as it was drunk ... As long as the barrel is kept full to the brim and the wine is not in contact with the air, the danger of it turning to vinegar is minimised.

La Part des Anges

ANOTHER POINT OF VIEW

So, 1640. Nine years before King Charles I is beheaded in front of Whitehall Palace. The fanatical puritan William Prynne writes to the King, protesting against the drinking of Royal Healths. (I quote this for the sake of Prohibitionist readers, who may feel that my book is biased against them. Which of course, it is.)

Most gracious and dread sovereign, in whose spiritual and corporal health and welfare, the safety, health and happiness both of our church and state subsist … Is not this a great affront, indignity and dishonour to your majesty, that your sacred health, your name, and royal crown should be thus profaned, and bandied up and down in every drunkard's mouth? In every cup and can? In every tavern, tap-house, hall or cellar? (unhallowed, base and sordid places, unworthy of so holy and great a name and presence); that every degenerous, infamous and stigmatical Belialist; every debased and brutish pot-companion, whose very company and acquaintance all christians should abhor; that the very scouring, dregs and scum of men should so far debase and undervalue them, as to prostitute them to their swinish sins and lusts; as if drunkenness were the sole and only faith that kings defend? Doubtless though it were the honour of heathen kings and devil-gods in former ages, to have their healths caroused and quaffed off at every solemn and festival meeting; yet it is the greatest contumely, indignity and dishonour to any good or christian king, who should be a very god on earth to have his name, his health, his crown and dignity thus vilified and abused; by sordid, beastly, wicked and ungodly men, to such sinister, sinful, graceless, heathenish and infernal ends as these; to patronise their gross intemperance, and so to drown their own and others' souls in drunkenness, riot and excess of wine.

Jesus, I need a drink!!! That incidentally is a heavily cut version, a mere fraction of what Prynne actually wrote. He was a man of passionate convictions.

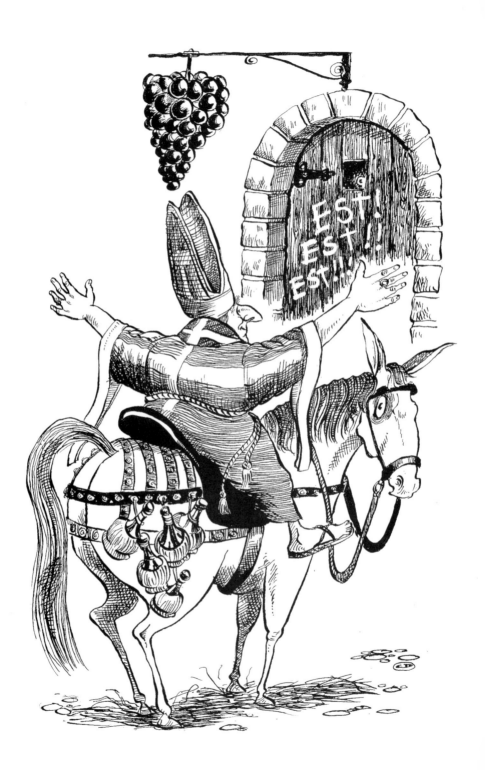

Back to the Steinwein. Back to Würzburg.

Having survived ... By the way it was from nearby Augsburg, that Bishop Johann Fugger set out on his journey to attend the coronation of the Holy Roman Emperor. This led to one of the most eccentrically named wines, *Est! Est!! Est!!!* The bishop sent his servant, Martin, ahead to find the inns that served the best wine (a sort of 12th century Egon Ronay, you might say) and to leave a sign outside, *Vinum bonum est.* The wine is good. Can you imagine? Martin had to stop off at every inn and sample the goods. He soon shortened his message to simply *Est.* When he reached Montefiascone, north of Rome, he thought the wine was terrific.

So good in fact that he chalked up on the door of the inn **Est!**

He drank another bottle. *Mmmm ... ja ja, gut gut ...* **Est!!**

And another. *Mein Gott, das ist wunderbar ...* **EST!!!**

And the name stuck, complete with exclamation marks.

They grow on trees

WHERE WOULD THEY BE WITHOUT THE ENGLISH?

Early 1700s. Having survived in barrel for a couple of centuries, the Steinwein of 1540 is finally bottled. Why the long delay? Waiting for corks and bottles.

The ancient Romans had invented a technique for blowing glass bottles. But they were light and fragile. It was the English in the 17th century who first made them robust. There was a timber shortage at the time, so we used coal-fired furnaces, which reached higher temperatures and made stronger bottles. Onion-shaped at first, with long necks, they later became cylindrical as we know them. For the first time glass bottles could be used for storing, even for long-distance transportation of wine.

Corks ... grow on trees. They're made from the bark of cork oaks which grow wild in the mountains of Spain and Portugal. They soon became the favoured bottle-stopper, being cheap and efficient. So, with the arrival of corks and bottles, the Steinwein can leave its barrel in the early 1700s. It then begins a further 200 years of gradual maturation.

Time for some more poetry.

O for a draught of vintage! that hath been
  Cool'd a long age in the deep-delved earth,
Tasting of Flora and the country green,
  Dance, and Provençal song, and sunburnt mirth!
O for a beaker full of the warm South,
  Full of the true, the blushful Hippocrene,
    With beaded bubbles winking at the brim,
      And purple-stained mouth;
    That I might drink, and leave the world unseen,
    And with thee fade away into the forest dim.
John Keats.

Wonderful idea, that wine should *taste* of dance, and Provençal
song, and sunburnt mirth.

THE BEAUTIFUL, BUBBLING BEVERAGE

But we were in the early 1700s. Champagne also becomes possible. Well, you can't have champagne without bottles and corks, can you? Wine maybe. Champagne, absolutely not.

In the middle ages the wine of Champagne was neither sparkling nor white. It was still and pale red, like an anaemic burgundy. Some still is. Bouzy Rouge for example, made in the Champagne village called 'Bouzy'.

There are many legends surrounding the famous champagne-making monk, Dom Pérignon. That he was blind; that his taste buds were so sensitive he could tell which field a single grape came from; that he said, prophetically, *'I'm drinking stars'*; that he was strangely, unmonkishly abstemious in his own drinking habits. And most importantly, that he was 'the man who invented champagne'. But that's a fairy tale. Dom Pérignon's wines didn't sparkle, and they weren't meant to. He tried to stop them bubbling. To him, refermentation was a damned nuisance, because it produced more carbon dioxide, which often broke the flimsy bottles. But he was a brilliant wine-maker. His main inspiration was blending: blending wines from many different vineyards; blending the three champagne grapes Chardonnay, Pinot Noir and Pinot Meunier; and blending different vintages.

The beautiful, bubbling beverage was first drunk by the English in the late 17th century. How so? Lemme tellya. Champagne is France's most northern wine region, it is north east of Paris. By the end of the grape harvest autumn is advancing, temperatures are cooling down, and fermentation *appears* to have stopped, as yeast doesn't work when it's too cold. The wine is shipped in barrels, and bottled in England. Spring arrives, temperatures warm up, and fermentation recommences, creating its by-product carbon dioxide. This would seep out of a barrel, but a closed bottle allows it no exit, so it lies waiting to emerge as fabulous frothy fizz.

Unless the bottle explodes.

Thanks to coal-fired furnaces, British glassmakers were making stronger bottles. But the pressure in a bottle of champagne is equal to the inside of a London bus tyre, and for many years the process remained hazardous. There were heavy losses, up to 50%. It was strongly advisable to wear iron masks in champagne cellars to avoid being lacerated by flying glass. I read about one cellar where three workmen had each lost an eye. But worry not. The hero of the hour was a young pharmacist called André François. In 1836 he published a formula enabling precise quantities of sugar and yeast to be added to induce the second fermentation in bottle, without also inducing an explosion. Finally champagne took off, after nearly 200 years of exploding bottles. Within a generation it was the world's first Wine Industry. And highly lucrative. A poor champagne grower, they say, is one who has to clean his own Rolls Royce.

The Cautious Cellarman

They'll pay later...

But tell me this, as a matter of interest. How do you get the dead yeast out of the bottle? It's the dead yeast that gives it that lovely biscuitty flavour. But if you leave it in, the wine is cloudy. And if you take too long, you lose the bubbles.

The second megastar of the region was Veuve Cliquot, 'the Widow'. She is credited with inventing *remuage*, or riddling. They say she cut 45 degree holes in her kitchen table. She stuck her bottles in, giving them a twist and shake every day for six weeks, gradually turning them upside down, until the dead yeast rested on the cork. After that it was just a matter of *dégorgement*: freezing the neck of the bottle, turning it back upright, removing the cap and standing clear as a pellet of yeasty ice hit the ceiling, rapidly inserting a champagne cork, et voilà! A crude definition, but essentially accurate.

The Widow was also a brilliant business-woman. When Russian troops were camped around Rheims in 1814, after forcing Napoleon's retreat from Moscow, they naturally looted her cellars. *'Let them drink,'* she said, *'they'll pay later.'* She proceeded to send salesmen to Moscow and St. Petersburg, cornering the market. One wrote back to her: *'The Tsarina is with child. If it is a Prince, gallons of champagne will be drunk in this vast country. Do not mention it, all our rivals would be here at once.'*

Champagne reached a peak of popularity during the Naughty Nineties, in the Paris of the Belle Époque. Maxims restaurant and The Folies Bergères were the places to go, and champagne tasted best when drunk from actresses' slippers.

A popular brand of the time was Champagne de la Jarretière. Champagne of the garter. They gave away a pair of garters with each bottle. The poster showed a gorgeous girl with plunging décolleté, neckband, and a huge twirl of feathers in her hair, smiling seductively and raising her petticoat to allow an ageing roué kneeling at her feet (that's my part) to slip a garter up her leg.

At a famous banquet given by the Marquis de Sillery, champagne was presented in baskets of flowers carried by young girls clad as 'Priestesses of Bacchus' ... whatever that may mean.

Lord Nelson, dining with Sir William and the stunningly beautiful Lady Hamilton, watched Emma drink enough champagne to lose her inhibitions, and favour the company with her imitations of classical statuary ... whatever that may mean.

Madame de Pompadour (one of the "Grandes Horizontales" ... and we all know what *that* means) declared: *'Champagne is the only wine that leaves a woman looking beautiful after drinking it.'*

Premier's
Cru

Winston Churchill is said to have enjoyed a drop, even for his breakfast. Even while holding high office. But the size of the drop was the subject of delicate negotiation. *'When I drink from a bottle, I'm happy,'* he said. *'When I drink from a half-bottle I'm not happy, but Clementine is happy. To make us both happy, I will drink Imperial Pints.'* Pol Roger was the Great Man's favourite champagne house. He even gave the name to his racehorse. He used to say: *'I am easily satisfied, with the best.'* Pol Roger returned the compliment by naming their prestige cuvée *Sir Winston Churchill*, sold only in magnums.

Madame Lily Bollinger, when asked how she enjoyed her own product, said: *'I drink it when I'm happy, and when I'm sad. Sometimes I drink it when I'm alone. When I have company, I consider it obligatory. I trifle with it if I'm not hungry and drink it when I am. Otherwise I never touch it ... unless I'm thirsty.'*

With all this talk about champagne, you probably think I've forgotten all about the Steinwein. But no. It is still there, lying in its cool, damp, dark cellar acquiring, let's hope, ever greater depth and complexity.

But it's nice to know, isn't it, that if it wasn't for the English pointing them in the right direction, the French would never have had the wit to invent champagne. We English don't bother to make much wine, but we've had our moments. Like owning Bordeaux for 300 years. When Eleanor of Aquitaine married our King Henry II, she gave him Bordeaux as her dowry. Those were the days, eh? I'll come back to that.

A DRINK FOR CRUSTY OLD FARTS?

But first, a brief Port Digression. (Another English discovery, of course.) It tastes so lip-smackingly delicious, and it has such wonderfully quaint rituals. And paraphenalia.

Tongs, for instance. With champagne the stylish way into a bottle is by *sabrage*. You literally decapitate the bottle with a sabre. David Gower is said to be an expert. But with port a rather less swashbuckling approach is adopted. If the cork is too old and crumbly to be drawn out in the usual way, the neck of the bottle may be gripped with red hot tongs, then immediately wrapped in a cold, damp cloth. The sudden change in temperature causes the neck to break clean off.

'All wine would be Port, if it could' is a favourite saying in the Port trade.

Traditionally the decanter circulates around the table in a clockwise direction. Should some scoundrel neglect to pass it on, there are various coded messages which may be sent down the table, such as *'Ahem … your passport is out of order!'* Or *'It's a very long ship!'* Or (my favourite) *'Are you a friend of the Bishop of Norwich?'*

Unlike champagne, port seems to invite gravitas, evoked here by the novelist George Meredith:

Having slowly ingurgitated and meditated upon this precious draught, and turned its flavour over and over with an attitude of potent judicial wisdom, the old lawyer heaved, and said, sharpening his lips over the admirable vintage, 'The world is in a very sad state, I fear, Sir Austin'. His client gazed at him queerly. 'But that', he added immediately, ill-concealing by his gaze the glowing intestinal congratulations going on within him, 'that is, I think you might say, Sir Austin, if I could but prevail upon you, a tolerably good character wine'.

An example of Careless Sabrage

THREE-BOTTLE MEN AND OTHERS
WITH PURPLE NOSES

In the 19th century the Steinwein makes a move. Its long sleep is briefly disturbed when the bottles pass into the cellars of Ludwig II of Bavaria ('Mad King Ludwig'), where they acquire labels featuring the Bavarian crown. They're later sold at auction to Gebrüder Simon, Wine Merchants in Wiesbaden, where an ever dwindling number lies for a further 50 years.

This was a period of colossal consumption, famous for massive drinking bouts, for 'Three-Bottle Men'. *'Is it true, sir, that you drank three bottles of port without assistance?'* - *'No sir, I had the help of a bottle of madeira.'* It must have been a helluva time for sore heads.

A colourful scene of debauchery is described in Lord Cockburn's Journal:

It was at Kilravock that old Henry Mackenzie used to tell that a sort of household officer was kept, whose duty was to prevent the drunk guests from choking. Mackenzie was once at a festival there, towards the close of which the exhausted topers sank gradually back and down on their chairs, till little of them was seen above the table except their noses; and at last they disappeared altogether and fell on the floor. Those who were too far gone to rise lay still there from necessity; while those who were glad of a pretence for escaping fell into a doze from policy. While Mackenzie was in this state he was alarmed by feeling a hand working about his throat, and called out. A voice answered 'Dinna be feared sir, it's me.' - 'And who are you?' - 'A'm the lad that louses the cravats.'

On a similar theme, here is the late Lord Wolfenden:

I had a case of whisky in my cellar and my wife told me to empty each and every bottle down the sink, or else … so I reluctantly proceeded with the unhappy task.

I drew the cork from the first bottle and poured the contents down the sink, with the exception of one glass, which I drank.

I pulled the cork from the second bottle and did likewise, with the exception of one glass, which I drank.

I emptied the third bottle, except for one glass, which I drank and then I took the cork from the fourth sink, poured the glass down the bottle and drank that too.

I pulled the bottle from the next glass, drank one sink out of it, and emptied the rest down the cork.

Then I pulled the sink from the next bottle and poured it down the glass and drank the cork, and finally I took the glass from the last bottle, emptied the cork, poured the sink down the rest and drank the pour.

When I had everything emptied, I steadied the house with one hand, counted the bottles and glasses and corks with the other, and found there were 29.

To make sure I recounted them, when they came by again, and this time there were 74.

As the house came around the next time I counted them again, and finally I had all the houses and sinks and glasses and corks and bottles counted, except one house, which I then drank.

Actually, it only takes one drink to get me loaded.
Trouble is, I can't remember if it's the 13th or the 14th.
George Burns.

Wine was created from the beginning to make men joyful,
and not to make them drunk.
Ecclesiastes.

A man is never drunk if he can lie on the floor without holding on.
Joe E. Lewis.

Rather~Merry~Go~Round

Bertram in need of a bracer

RED HOT SPIKES IN THE HEAD

Truly, sir, and pleasure will be paid, one time or another.
William Shakespeare.

*I reached out a hand from under the blankets, and rang the bell for Jeeves.
'Good evening, Jeeves'. 'Good morning, sir'.
This surprised me. 'Is it morning?' 'Yes, sir'.
'Are you sure? It seems very dark outside'.
'There is a fog, sir. If you will recollect, we are now in Autumn - season
of mists and mellow fruitfulness'.
'Season of what?'
'Mists, sir, and mellow fruitfulness'.
'Oh? Yes. Yes, I see. Well, be that as it may, get me one of those bracers
of yours, will you?'
'I have one in readiness, sir, in the ice-box'.
He shimmered out, and I sat up in bed with that rather unpleasant feeling
you get sometimes that you're going to die in about 5 minutes. On the
previous night, I had given a little dinner at the Drones to Gussie Fink-
Nottle as a friendly send-off before his approaching nuptials with Madeline,
only daughter of Sir Watkyn Bassett, CBE, and these things take their toll.
Indeed, just before Jeeves came in, I had been dreaming that some bounder
was driving spikes through my head - not just ordinary spikes, as used by
Jael the wife of Heber, but red hot ones.
He returned with the tissue-restorer. I loosed it down the hatch, and after
undergoing the passing discomfort, unavoidable when you drink Jeeves's
patent morning revivers, of having the top of the skull fly up to the ceiling
and the eyes shoot out of their sockets and rebound from the opposite wall
like racquet balls, felt better. It would have been overstating it to say that
even now Bertram was back again in mid-season form, but I had at least
slid into the convalescent class and was equal to a spot of conversation.
'Ha!' I said, retrieving the eyeballs and replacing them in position. 'Well,
Jeeves, what goes on in the great world?'*
P.G.Wodehouse.

Back to the Steinway. Bechstein. What's it called? Pull yourself together, for heaven's sake. *Steinwein.* Last heard of, if I remember correctly, in the cellars of Gebrüder Simon, or Simon Brothers, in Wiesbaden. Now hear this, a tale of intrepidity and derring-do: in 1936, Nazi forces re-occupy the Rhineland, and Oscar Simon sleeps easier, having moved his family to England. He longs to do likewise for the remaining Steinwein. By great good fortune, he is friendly with Lady Betty Campbell, mother of water-speed ace Sir Donald Campbell, and a woman of remarkable pluck. She drives across Europe in an open-topped Bentley, her mission being the liberation of Jews from Hitler's Germany. She returns to England with a carload of Jewish teenagers, and the legendary wine stowed behind the seat. She deposits it for safe keeping in the City of London. Not so safe, as it turns out, for the premises are soon bombed during the blitz. The Steinwein is presumed destroyed.

Some 20 years later, Oscar Simon is dead. His son Henry is in Ehrmann's, the Wine Merchants in Grafton Street. There he sees a small, glass-fronted wine box, containing ancient bottles just like those thought lost in the blitz. Ehrmanns say they were bought at auction, but have no documentation to prove it. Henry Simon believes they are his, by inheritance. He adds that if he is correct, there will be, on the back of the box, the name and address of his grandfather's firm in Wiesbaden. This he writes down in a sealed envelope. They turn the box around. Nothing can be seen. But on closer examination by infra-red torch ... there, written with an ink pencil in ancient German script, is the address: *Gebrüder Simon, Nicolasstrasse 9, Wiesbaden.* Ehrmann's agree that they must indeed be Henry Simon's long lost bottles. How they got there, no-one knows.

Time perhaps to open the Steinwein? ... It'll have to wait just a tad longer. I haven't finished with Bordeaux yet.

Work is the curse of the drinking classes.
Oscar Wilde.

A Case of Identity

FROM SWAMPY PROMONTORY TO THE WORLD'S GREATEST

In the middle ages, when England owned Bordeaux for 300 years, the wine was called *clairet*, hence claret. It was a clear, light red wine for early drinking. No corks and bottles yet.

It was in the reign of the Sun King, Louis XIV, that Arnaud de Pontac produced Bordeaux's first top quality wine. His estate was Château Haut-Brion. Samuel Pepys wrote: *'Drank a sort of French wine, called Ho Bryan, that hath a good and most particular taste that I ever met with.'*

Venture capitalists began raising their noses to the wind. Inspired by de Pontac, they were soon pouring money into the region, looking for cheap land to develop. They found a long swampy promontory, described as *'sauvage et solitaire'* between the Gironde estuary and the Atlantic, called ... the Médoc. They cleared the swamps, drained the land and planted vineyards.

Around 1700 the famous Médoc châteaux begin to emerge. A great swell of the time was the Marquis de Ségur. Besides Château Calon-Ségur, he also owned the neighbouring Pauillac estates of Latour, Lafite and Mouton. Louis XV called him 'the Prince of Vines'. One day at court the king remarked upon his beautiful coat buttons: were they diamonds? *'No sire'*, replied the Marquis, *'they are much more precious, they are stones from my vineyard.'* His wines were soon selling for many times the price of ordinary Bordeaux, causing more money to flood into the region and more planting of vines.

By the mid-19th century Bordeaux's pre-eminent reputation was firmly established. It was formalised by the 1855 classification. This ranked the finest châteaux of the Médoc and the Graves into a hierarchy based on price. These châteaux produce fabulous, aristocratic, cabernet sauvignon-dominated wines, with intense blackcurrant and cedarwood flavours. The classification still holds good, more or less. It doesn't encourage shooting stars. Not on the left bank, at least.

But nowadays for the headiest delights, you must cross the Gironde estuary, slap your wallet on the table, and sample the truly voluptuous, merlot-based wines of St. Émilion and Pomerol. Here, *The times they are a-changin'*. New words are entering the vocabulary. Words like 'garagiste' and 'micro-cuvée'. They refer to the nineties phenomenon of super-concentrated wines, made in minute quantities and sold for rhino-stoppingly large sums of money. Le Pin, Valandraud and La Mondotte are three of the rarest, sexiest and most opulent of the millennium cuvées. But new ones appear like mushrooms overnight, and effortlessly outprice the Lafites and Latours of the Médoc. They are cousins of the "Boutique Wines" of California, where a 6 litre bottle of Screaming Eagle recently fetched $500,000 (I'll say that again, half a million dollars) at a Napa Valley charity auction.

One other superlative wine of Bordeaux, mentioned all too briefly, is Château d'Yquem. The great sweet, white wine, made with nobly rotten grapes. Curious expression, noble rot. The grapes develop a friendly fungus which concentrates their juice, leaving them shrivelled and ashen. Not a pretty sight. When a load of fruit is emptied into the press, instead of the usual squelching and running of juice, a cloud of dust arises. Each vine produces just one glass of wine. But it is Wine for the Gods!

Château d'Yquem. It brings me, not a moment too soon, to:

FATAL AGITATION

THE WINE AND SEX DIGRESSION

Concerning the legendary 1921 Yquem. Cyril Ray tells of a sexy young wife and her elderly husband, she merrily shagging her way through a nearby regiment, and he remarkably tolerant ... until one fateful occasion: *She was turned out at little more than a moment's notice, and divorced as quickly as a lady could. It was long before she could understand why. Why that evening, and not on any other? Finally it dawned on her. Until then, she had dispensed her favours in boudoir or in bedroom. But on that fateful evening she was showing off the house to a dashing young officer, and they had reached the wine cellar. A look in his hostess's eye had overwhelmed the boy; his ardour would not wait; and they were heard, and thus discovered, in such a position, she shyly intimated, as to be agitating the bin of Yquem 1921 ...* ('Yquem, Ysaw, Yconquered,' he no doubt cried).

Wine and sex, it's a rich vein.

Alcohol is like love: the first kiss is magic, the second is intimate, the third is routine. After that, you just take the girl's clothes off.
Raymond Chandler.

Candy is dandy, but liquor is quicker.
Ogden Nash.

I love to drink Martinis/Two at the very most.
Three, and I'm under the table/Four, and I'm under the host!
Dorothy Parker.

I was in love with a beautiful blonde once. She drove me to drink.
That's the one thing I'm indebted to her for.
W.C.Fields.

The breasts of a barmaid from Sale
Were tattooed with the prices of ale.
And on her behind/For the sake of the blind,
Was the same information in Braille.

No matter what you call it, it ruins many a plan;
It's Brewer's Droop in Bradford, and Coq-au-Vin in Cannes.

IN CONCLUSION

Time to return to the saga of the Sleeping Beauty. The truly venerable bottle. Having been smuggled out of Nazi Germany and miraculously survived bombing in the blitz, the Steinwein reappears mysteriously in Ehrmann's in Grafton Street. A bottle of the legendary vintage which should have been way over the hill by the time Beethoven was born, was reckoned to be at long last approaching its prime, and was finally opened in London on July 7th, 1961. Hugh Johnson was among the select few who were present.

He tells how two other fine 19th century German wines were opened first. A bottle of Schloss Johannisberger vintage 1820, and an 1857 Rüdesheimer. Both had turned out to be far, far too old. Not a trace of the taste of wine was left. They actually smelt of corruption.

All hopes now rested on the Steinwein. Imagine the hush of expectation. Imagine the infinite care with which the ancient cork is extracted, the intake of breath as it emerges, mouths dry in anticipation. Imagine the deft, rapid pouring, in the knowledge that whatever life it retains must be brief once it makes contact with the air.

The Steinwein was still wine. Dark brown, madeira-like, Germanic. Feeble, but quite definitely alive for two or three minutes ... before disintegrating and turning to bitter vinegar in their glasses. After 421 years. The briefest of brief glimpses back across the centuries to that baking hot, far distant summer of 1540.

When Tut'ankhamun's tomb was opened, they found wreaths of fresh flowers, which likewise crumbled to dust upon contact with the air. After 3000 years.

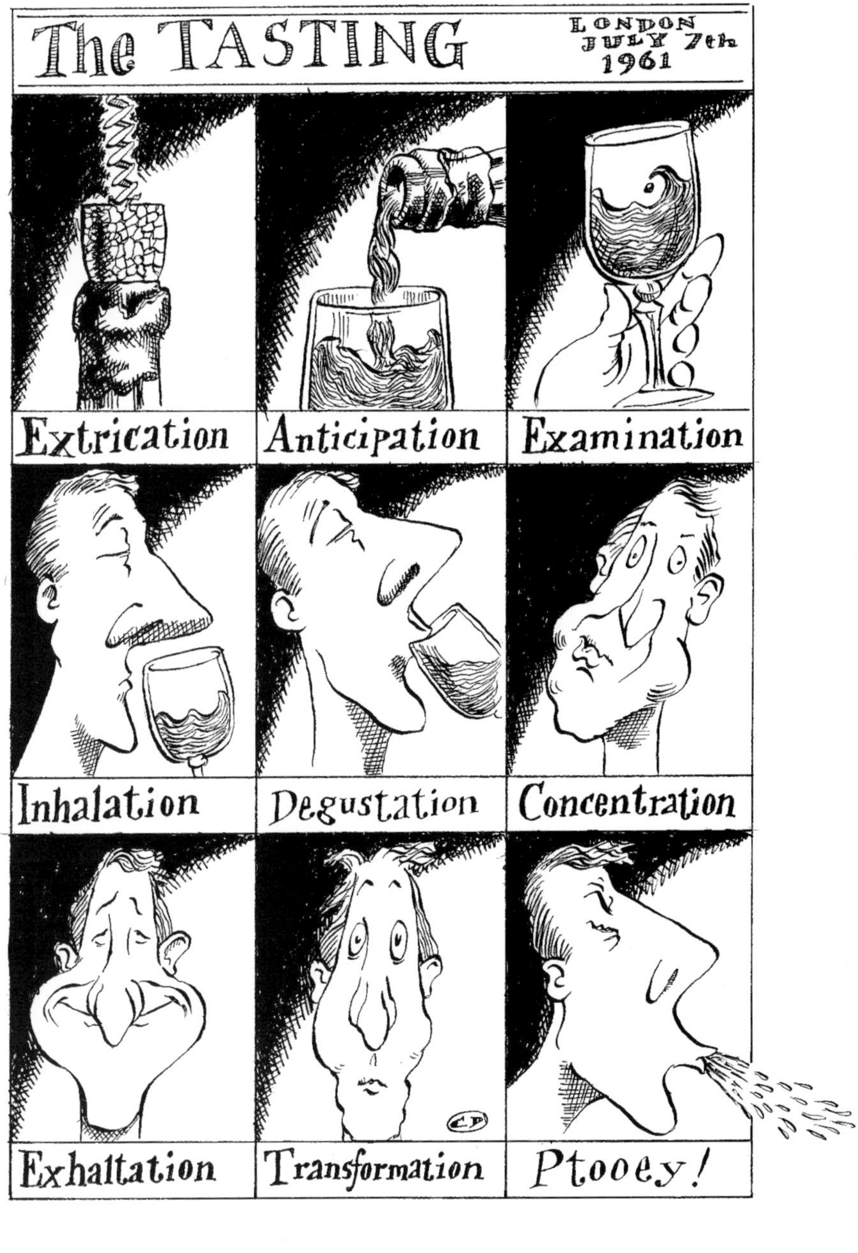
The TASTING
LONDON JULY 7th 1961
Extrication
Anticipation
Examination
Inhalation
Degustation
Concentration
Exhaltation
Transformation
Ptooey!

My friends should drink a dozen of claret on my tomb.
John Keats.

The point of drinking wine, Rumpole, is to taste sunlight trapped in a bottle, and to remember some stony slope in Tuscany, or a village by the Gironde.
Claude Erskine-Brown, with a little help from **John Mortimer.**

The great Irish humourist and drinker Myles na gCopaleen died on April Fool's Day 1966. John Ryan was at his funeral, with Patrick Kavanagh:

'Do you know the last thing he said?' Paddy asked me, coming out of the church.
'I don't', I replied.
'When he was lying in bed in the hospital, some fella brought him a naggin of gin and a baby tonic. He filled Myles' glass with the entire contents of the gin, adding about half a thimbleful of tonic. "Almighty God," Myles gasped, "Are you trying to drown it entirely?"' He swallowed his drink and dropped dead.

Ladies and gentlemen, your very good health.

Julian Curry unites his love of wine and theatre in *Hic!* As an actor, he is well known to TV audiences as Claude Erskine-Brown in the popular series *Rumpole of the Bailey*. He also has wide-ranging stage and screen credits, including leading roles with the RSC, the National and in the West End. His favourites include Angelo, Captain Brazen, Billy Rice, and Herrenstein in

Photograph by: John Halliday

Thomas Bernhart's *Elizabeth II*; also the entire cast of Samuel Beckett's *Company*. On TV *Inspector Morse, Sherlock Holmes, The Misanthrope, King Lear, Kavanagh QC, The Wyvern Mystery, The Hunt* and *The Cappuccino Years*. And on film *The Missionary, Fall from Grace, Loch Ness, Rasputin, Seven Days to Live* and John Huston's *Escape to Victory*. This last, a classic 'Golden Turkey', nonetheless involved the very great thrill of working with Pele. Julian is also an ardent wine buff of many years standing, and holds a Diploma from the Wine and Spirit Education Trust.

Chris Duggan studied painting at St. Martin's School of Art and at Goldsmith's College, before becoming a freelance illustrator and cartoonist. His work has appeared in The Times, The Daily Telegraph, Radio Times, The Independent and Punch, and he is a regular contributor to the Financial Times. He has been awarded the TUC prize for best illustration. A favourite

among Chris' previous books is *The Ascent of Rum Doodle* by W.E.Bowman. He has exhibited at the Showroom Gallery, and had his first one-man show at the Coningsby Gallery in London's West End. Chris lives and works in south east London, where he keeps a large collection of corks.